sushi

p

This is a Parragon Publishing Book
First published in 2004

Parragon Publishing
Queen Street House
4 Queen Street
Bath BA1 1HE, UK

ISBN: 1-40543-650-6

Printed in China

Produced by the Bridgewater Book Company Ltd.
Project Designer: Michael Whitehead
Project Editor: Anna Samuels
Photographer: David Jordan
Home Economist: Jacqueline Bellefontaine

Notes for the Reader
This book uses imperial, metric, or US cup measurements. Follow
the same units of measurement throughout; do not mix imperial
and metric. All spoon measurements are level: teaspoons are
assumed to be 5 ml, and tablespoons are assumed to be 15 ml.
Unless otherwise stated, eggs and individual vegetables are
medium, and pepper is freshly ground black pepper.

Recipes using raw or very lightly cooked eggs should be avoided by
infants, the elderly, pregnant women, convalescents, and anyone
suffering from an illness.

contents

introduction

SUSHI is a Japanese dish of small cakes of cold rice, traditionally with fish or vegetables, served with a vinegar sauce, pickles, and *wasabi* (Japanese horseradish). It is rapidly gaining in popularity outside Japan and the wide range of delicious recipes included in this book explains why.

Surprisingly, very little equipment is actually needed to make sushi. A special bamboo mixing tub (*hangiri* or *sushi-oke*) would be useful, as would a pressing box (*oshi waku*) and a rice spatula (*shamoji*). However, none of the mentioned items is really essential. A sushi mat (*makisu*) is really the only piece of equipment that you will need and this can be found in most Japanese stores or a good cook store.

Sushi is made using both raw and cooked fish. If you use raw fish, this is at your own risk. Raw fish has more bacteria and parasites than cooked fish. Some diseases, such as diabetes and liver disease, preclude you from eating raw fish or shellfish. Please consult your physician if in doubt. Mercury levels also tend to be higher in long-lived, larger fish with darker meat, such as swordfish,

king mackerel, and tuna. Pregnant women, nursing mothers, and young children should avoid eating these types of fish.

If you use raw fish, buy it from a good supplier or store that sells "sushi or sashimi grade" fish. Buy shellfish that comes from certified water and, once bought, refrigerate it immediately and use on the same day. Prepare everything else before taking the fish out of the refrigerator, keeping everything very clean, and serve immediately.

Included in this book are tasty recipes for fish and seafood sushi, meat and poultry sushi, and rice, vegetables, and tempura. There are four types of sushi dishes, which are made and presented differently: boat sushi, rolled sushi, pressed sushi, and scattered sushi.

BOAT SUSHI

Boat sushi dishes are made by wrapping *nori* (paper-thin sheets of dried seaweed) around molded rice and are excellent for serving toppings such as fish roe or softer toppings such as tuna mayonnaise.

ROLLED SUSHI

Rolling sushi (*maki-zushi*) is a very popular way of making sushi and does not require a huge amount of practice in order to master the technique. A sheet of nori is spread with rice and fillings and rolled up. The roll is then cut into small pieces, which are served with the cut side up so that the varied and colorful fillings can be seen. Thin or fatter rolls can be cut and only a small amount of filling is necessary. A sushi roll can also be served

whole. When the rolls are made, they need to be cut with a very sharp and slightly dampened knife so that the rice does not stick. The rolls can be served with soy sauce, mayonnaise, or sweet chili sauce and can be presented on square or rectangular plates with pickled ginger and wasabi.

PRESSED SUSHI

This is one of the easiest types of sushi. Pressed sushi and box sushi (*oshi-zushi* and *hako-zushi* respectively) are made in a three-piece bamboo pressing box (*oshi waku*), though a pan with a loose bottom or a terrine mold with drop-down sides is fine. If you have fixed-base pans, the sushi has to be made upside down: toppings are placed in the pan first and the rice is pressed on top, then the sushi is turned out. Wait a few minutes to let the flavors develop again before cutting the sushi, using a very sharp knife wiped damp between each cut so that the rice does not stick.

SCATTERED SUSHI

Scattered sushi (*chirashi-zushi*), like pressed sushi, is very easy to make. A pretty serving bowl for each person is key, as presentation of this food is important. Toppings are suggested in this book but you can mix and match toppings according to your own tastes. Add pickled ginger and wasabi to the topping as a garnish or serve them separately in little bowls alongside the soy sauce and Japanese mayonnaise for dipping.

fish sushi

A WIDE selection of fish can be used to make sushi, each dish as beautiful and delicious as the next. The recipes included in Part One are very varied, from sushi boats to rolled, pressed, and scattered sushi using fish such as salmon, tuna, cod, eel, mackerel, and trout.

salmon roe sushi boats

Roe is often used for making sushi. Most roe used is orange, either large salmon or trout roe or tiny flying fish roe. It can be bought in jars. **MAKES 8 PIECES**

⅓ quantity freshly cooked sushi rice
(see page 78)
2 small sheets of toasted nori, each cut into
4 strips lengthwise
wasabi paste
8 tbsp salmon, trout, or flying fish roe

Divide the rice into 8 batches. Dampen your hands to stop the rice sticking, then shape each batch of the rice into an oval using your hands. Carefully wrap a strip of nori around each piece of rice and trim off any excess, then stick together at the join using a couple of crushed grains of rice.

Dab a little wasabi on top of each sushi boat and top with a tablespoon of the salmon roe. Serve the sushi straightaway with soy sauce on the side.

to serve

soy sauce

salmon, spinach & wasabi mash rolls

Use good all-purpose or mashing potatoes like King Edwards or Desirée for this recipe. You want a smooth, thick mash so the filling stays solid and rolls easily. *MAKES 24 PIECES*

2 large potatoes, peeled and cut into fourths
1 scallion, finely chopped
wasabi paste
salt
4 oz/115 g sushi-grade salmon
or piece of salmon fillet
1 tbsp oil
6 small sheets of toasted nori
handful of spinach leaves, stems removed

Cook the potatoes in a pan of boiling salted water for 20–30 minutes, or until tender. Mash, then mix them with the scallion and enough wasabi to give the potatoes a bit of a kick. Season with salt to taste. Chill for 30 minutes, or until the mash is very firm.

If using the salmon fillet, pull the skin off and remove any bones. Heat the oil in a skillet and cook the salmon over medium heat, on both sides, for 8 minutes, or until it is cooked through. Cool and cut the sushi/cooked salmon into strips.

Divide the mash into 6 equal portions. Put a sheet of nori shiny-side down on a rolling mat with the longest end toward you and mound 1 portion of the mash on the bottom third of the nori. Lay a sixth of the spinach leaves on top, then a layer of salmon.

To roll the sushi, fold the mat over, starting at the end where the ingredients are and tucking in the end of the nori to start the roll. Keep rolling, lifting up the mat as you go and keeping the pressure even but gentle until you have finished the roll. Moisten the top edge of the nori with water to seal the sushi roll closed.

Remove the roll from the mat and cut it into 4 even-size pieces with a wet, very sharp knife. Turn the pieces on end and then arrange them on a plate. Repeat with the remaining ingredients.

to serve

shoyu (Japanese soy sauce)

wasabi paste

pickled ginger

seven-spiced salmon rolls

Sichimi togarashi is a seven-spice mix usually containing red pepper, sansho pepper, sesame seeds, flax seeds, poppy seeds, ground nori, and dried, ground tangerine peel. *MAKES 24 PIECES*

5¹/₂-oz/150-g piece of salmon fillet
sichimi togarashi (seven-spice powder)
chili flakes
1 tbsp oil
1 quantity freshly cooked sushi rice
(see page 78)
6 small sheets of toasted nori
2 tbsp Japanese mayonnaise

Pull the skin off the salmon fillet and remove any bones. Dust the surface heavily with *sichimi togarashi* and sprinkle over a few chili flakes. Heat the oil in a skillet and cook the salmon over medium heat on both sides for 8 minutes, or until cooked through. Cool and flake into large pieces.

Divide the rice into 6 equal portions. Put a sheet of nori shiny-side down on a rolling mat with the longest end toward you. Using wet hands, spread 1 portion of the rice in an even layer on the nori, leaving 3/4 inch/2 cm of nori visible at the end farthest away from you. Don't squash the rice or make the layer too thick—you should be able to see the nori through the rice.

Spread the mayonnaise onto the rice at the end nearest you. Lay a sixth of the salmon on top of the mayonnaise.

To roll the sushi, fold the mat over, starting at the end where the ingredients are and tucking in the end of the nori to start the roll. Keep rolling, lifting up the mat as you go and keeping the pressure even but gentle until you have finished the roll. Moisten the top edge of the nori with water to seal the sushi roll closed.

Remove the roll from the mat and cut it into 4 even-size pieces with a wet, very sharp knife. Turn the pieces on end and arrange them on a plate. Repeat with the remaining ingredients. Serve with shoyu, wasabi, and pickled ginger.

sweet chili
salmon hand rolls

Sweet chili sauce is available in many different brands. The best are Thai brands, available from Chinese and Thai stores. *MAKES 6 PIECES*

Season the piece of salmon with the salt and pepper. Heat the oil in a skillet until it is very hot, then add the salmon skin-side down. Cook for 2 minutes, or until the skin is very crisp, then turn the heat down to medium and cook for an additional 2 minutes. Turn the salmon over and cook for an additional minute, or until it is cooked through. Let cool, then flake the salmon, keeping some pieces attached to the crispy skin.

Lay a piece of nori out on the counter and put some rice on the sheet. Spread the rice out evenly so that it takes up the bottom two-thirds of the sheet. Lay a sixth of the salmon, salmon skin, and scallion on the rice, then drizzle over a little mayonnaise and dot on a tiny amount of sweet chili sauce. Roll the nori into a cone, folding the bottom corner in as you roll. You will have to paste the join together with a couple of crushed grains of rice. Repeat with the other pieces of nori. Garnish with cucumber batons.

5¹/₂-oz/150-g piece of salmon fillet, skin on

salt and pepper

1 tbsp oil

3 large sheets of toasted nori, halved

¹/₄ quantity freshly cooked sushi rice
    (see page 78)

2 scallions, halved and shredded

4 tbsp Japanese mayonnaise

2 tbsp sweet chili sauce

to garnish

cucumber batons

salmon, asparagus & mayonnaise rolls

Japanese mayonnaise is also called "kewpie mayonnaise" because of the kewpie doll logo used by the company. It usually comes in a plastic bottle within a bag printed with a kewpie doll outline. You can use ordinary mayonnaise instead, though a whole-egg mayonnaise will taste better, as it tends to be less vinegary or sweet. *MAKES 24 PIECES*

6 asparagus spears

5¹/₂ -oz/150-g piece of salmon fillet or the same amount of sushi-grade salmon, cut into batons

1 tbsp oil

1 quantity freshly cooked sushi rice (see page 78)

6 small sheets of toasted nori

wasabi paste

1 tbsp Japanese mayonnaise

1 tsp toasted sesame seeds

Lay the asparagus spears flat in a skillet filled with simmering water and cook until tender when pierced with the tip of a knife. Cut into 3¹/₂-inch/ 9-cm lengths and let cool.

If using the salmon fillet, pull the skin off and remove any bones. Heat the oil in a skillet and cook the salmon over medium heat on both sides for 8 minutes, or until it is cooked through. Cool and flake into large pieces.

Divide the rice into 6 equal portions. Put a sheet of nori shiny-side down on a rolling mat with the longest end toward you. Using wet hands, spread 1 portion of the rice in an even layer on the nori, leaving 3/4 inch/2 cm of nori visible at the end farthest away from you. Spread a small amount of wasabi onto the rice at the end nearest you,

then spread on the mayonnaise. Lay an asparagus spear on top of the mayonnaise, then put some of the salmon next to it. Sprinkle the sesame seeds on top.

To roll the sushi, fold the mat over, starting at the end where the ingredients are and tucking in the end of the nori to start the roll. Keep rolling, lifting up the mat as you go and keeping the pressure even but gentle until you have finished the roll. Moisten the top edge of the nori with water to seal the sushi roll closed.

Remove the roll from the mat and cut it into 4 even-size pieces with a wet, very sharp knife. Turn the pieces on end and arrange them on a plate. Repeat with the remaining ingredients. Serve with shoyu and pickled ginger.

to serve
shoyu (Japanese soy sauce)
pickled ginger

to serve

pickled ginger

wasabi paste

salmon, lemon mayonnaise & avocado pressed sushi bars

Oshi waku are wooden boxes made for pressing sushi. They consist of a frame plus a removable lid and base and come in different sizes. *MAKES 8–10 PIECES*

1/2 quantity freshly cooked sushi rice
(see page 78)
2 tbsp Japanese mayonnaise
2 tsp lemon zest
5¹/2 oz/150 g smoked salmon
1 large ripe avocado, cut into thin batons

Oil an *oshi waku* or terrine mold (preferably with drop-down sides), then line it with a piece of plastic wrap so that the plastic wrap hangs over the edges. This is to help you pull the sushi out afterward. Pack the mold 1¹/4 inches/3 cm full with the rice. Mix the mayonnaise with the lemon zest and spread a layer of mayonnaise on top of the rice. Arrange the smoked salmon and avocado in thick, diagonal strips on top of the rice. Cover the top of the rice with a strip of plastic wrap, then put another terrine mold on top and weight down with something heavy, such as a couple of cans of tomatoes.

Chill the sushi for 15 minutes, then take off the mold and weights and pull out the sushi. Cut the sushi into 8–10 pieces with a wet, sharp knife. Serve with pickled ginger and wasabi paste.

pressed sushi
with smoked salmon
& cucumber

Smoked salmon makes a good ingredient in sushi because of its texture. You can buy a piece of fillet and slice it yourself if you want thicker slices. *MAKES 8–10 PIECES*

¹/₂ quantity freshly cooked sushi rice
(see page 78)
2 tbsp Japanese mayonnaise
7 oz/200 g smoked salmon
¹/₂ cucumber, peeled and cut into
very thin slices

to serve
pickled ginger
wasabi paste

Use a conventional wooden or plastic *oshi waku* or oil a terrine mold and line it with a piece of plastic wrap so that the plastic wrap hangs over the edges. This is to help you pull the sushi out afterward. Pack the mold 1¹/₄ inches/3 cm full with the rice. Spread a layer of mayonnaise on top of the rice. Arrange the smoked salmon and cucumber in diagonal strips on top of the rice, doubling up the salmon if you have enough so that the topping is nice and thick. Cover the top of the rice with a strip of plastic wrap, then put another terrine mold on top and weight down with something heavy, such as a couple of cans of tomatoes.

Chill the sushi for 15 minutes, then take off the mold and weights and pull out the sushi. Cut the sushi into 8–10 pieces with a wet, sharp knife. Serve with pickled ginger and wasabi paste.

to serve
pickled ginger
wasabi paste

cod goujon hand rolls
with tartare sauce

Tartare sauce can be easily bought—just look for a premium brand based on a whole-egg mayonnaise for the best flavor. If you don't like tartare sauce, use mayonnaise with this recipe. *MAKES 6 PIECES*

6 cod or haddock goujons
3 large sheets of toasted nori, halved
¹/₄ quantity freshly cooked sushi rice
(see page 78)
3 tbsp tartare sauce, plus extra to serve
3 scallions, halved and shredded

Cook the fish goujons according to the package directions. Cool them, then cut them into 1¹/₂-inch/4-cm pieces.

Lay a piece of nori out on the counter and put some rice on the sheet. Spread the rice out evenly so that it takes up the bottom two-thirds of the sheet. Spread a little of the tartare sauce onto the rice and top with a sixth of the goujons and scallion. Roll the nori into a cone, folding the bottom corner in as you roll. You will have to paste the join together with a couple of crushed grains of rice. Repeat with the other pieces of nori. Serve with pickled ginger, wasabi paste and extra tartare sauce for dipping.

glazed eel hand rolls

The eel (*unagi*) used for sushi has a soy, sake, and mirin glaze brushed over it
before cooking. You can buy glazed eel from Japanese stores, or you can use smoked eel fillets,
which may be easier to find. *MAKES 6 PIECES*

Put the soy sauce, mirin, and sake in a pan and
simmer for 5 minutes, or until slightly thickened.
Stir in a teaspoon of honey, then taste, adding
more honey until the sauce is sweet enough
for your taste.

Lay out a piece of nori on the counter and put
some rice on the sheet. Spread the rice out evenly
so that it takes up the bottom two-thirds of the
sheet. Lay a sixth of the eel over the rice and
drizzle the eel and rice liberally with the sauce.
Add a couple of slices of avocado. Roll the nori into
a cone, folding the bottom corner in as you roll. You
will have to paste the join together with a couple
of crushed grains of rice. Repeat with the other
pieces of nori.

^{1}/2 cup soy sauce

2 tbsp mirin

2 tbsp sake

honey, to taste

3 large sheets of toasted nori, halved

^{1}/4 quantity freshly cooked sushi rice
(see page 78)

2 smoked eel fillets, cut into strips lengthwise

^{1}/2 ripe avocado, cut into slices

scattered sushi
with smoked mackerel

Daikon is a long, white radish that has a crisp white flesh and a peppery flavor.
It goes well with fish and is often used as a garnish. *SERVES 4*

8 snow peas

2-inch/5-cm piece of daikon

1 quantity freshly cooked sushi rice

(see page 78)

juice and zest of 1 lemon

2 scallions, finely chopped

2 smoked mackerel, skin removed and

cut into diagonal strips

1/2 cucumber, peeled and cut into slices

Cook the snow peas in boiling, salted water for 1 minute. Drain and put aside to cool. Shred the daikon using the finest setting on a mandoline or a very sharp knife. If you are using a knife, cut the daikon into long, thin slices and cut each slice along its length as finely as you can.

Mix the sushi rice with the lemon juice and lemon zest.

Divide the rice between 4 wooden or ceramic bowls—they should be about 3/4 inch/2 cm full. Scatter the scallion over the top. Arrange the mackerel, cucumber, snow peas, and daikon on top of the rice. Garnish with pickled ginger and a small mound of wasabi.

to garnish

pickled ginger

wasabi paste

to serve
Ponzu Sauce (see page 48)
chopped radish with toasted sesame seeds

smoked trout
sushi boats

Smoked trout can be bought as fillets or as whole trout.
The whole trout often have a more pronounced flavor. *MAKES 8 PIECES*

**¹/₃ quantity freshly cooked sushi rice
(see page 78)
2 small sheets of toasted nori, each cut into
4 strips lengthwise
2 tbsp Japanese mayonnaise**

**1 tsp grated lemon zest
2 tsp lemon juice
2 scallions, finely chopped
1 smoked trout fillet, flaked
2 oz/55 g smoked salmon, cut into strips**

Divide the rice into 8 batches. Dampen your hands
to stop the rice sticking, then shape each batch of
the rice into an oval using your hands. Carefully
wrap a strip of nori around each piece of rice and
trim off any excess, then stick together at the join
using a couple of crushed grains of rice.

Mix the mayonnaise with the lemon zest and
juice and spread a little on top of each sushi boat.
Sprinkle with some scallion, then top with some of
the smoked trout and smoked salmon. Serve the
sushi straightaway with Ponzu Sauce and chopped
radish with toasted sesame seeds.

teriyaki tuna pressed sushi with green bean strips

Pickled ginger slices are used to cleanse the palate in between eating different types of sushi. Pickled ginger can be bought in bags and is often a bright pink color. *MAKES 15 PIECES*

**7 oz/200 g sushi-grade tuna or tuna fillet,
thinly sliced**

2 tbsp teriyaki sauce

1 tbsp oil

10 green beans, trimmed and cut in half

oil, for frying

1 tsp toasted sesame seeds

**1/2 quantity freshly cooked sushi rice
(see page 78)**

2 tbsp Japanese mayonnaise

Coat the tuna slices in the teriyaki sauce and cook in the oil in a skillet for 1 minute on each side. Then cut them into thick strips. Blanch the green beans in boiling water for a minute, then cool under cold running water and drain.

Oil an *oshi waku* or 7-inch/18-cm loose-bottomed square cake pan and line it with a piece of plastic wrap so that the plastic wrap hangs over the edges. This is to help you pull the sushi out afterward. Oil the plastic wrap and scatter in the sesame seeds. Pack the pan 1¼ inches/3 cm full with the rice. Spread a layer of mayonnaise on top. Arrange the tuna and green beans in thick, diagonal strips over the rice. Cover the top of the rice with a strip of plastic wrap, then put another cake pan on top and weight down with something heavy, such as a couple of cans of tomatoes.

Let the sushi chill for about 15 minutes, then take off the pan and weights, loosen the sides of the pan and pull out the sushi. Cut the sushi into about 15 pieces with a wet, sharp knife. Serve with pickled ginger and wasabi paste.

to serve

pickled ginger

wasabi paste

tuna tataki hand rolls

Hand rolls can be made in different sizes. They should ideally be big enough to need several bites, but you can make smaller cocktail-size rolls if you prefer. *MAKES 6 PIECES*

1 tsp black pepper

1 tbsp grated fresh ginger

1 tbsp sesame seeds

5¹/₂ oz/150 g sushi-grade tuna
    or very fresh tuna fillet

salt

2 tbsp oil

3 large sheets of toasted nori, halved

¹/₄ quantity freshly cooked sushi rice
    (see page 78)

¹/₂ cucumber, cut into batons

4 tbsp Japanese mayonnaise

wasabi paste

Mix the black pepper, ginger, and sesame seeds together and rub them all over the tuna, pressing the seeds on firmly. Season the tuna lightly with salt. Heat the oil in a skillet until it is very hot. Sear the tuna on all sides for 6 minutes, or until it is almost cooked through—keep pressing it until it feels firm. Remove from the skillet and cool, then slice into thin slices. Lay out a piece of nori on the counter and put some rice on the sheet.

Spread the rice out evenly so that it takes up the bottom two-thirds of the sheet.

Lay a sixth of the tuna and cucumber on the rice, then drizzle over a little mayonnaise and dot on a tiny amount of wasabi. Roll the nori into a cone, folding the bottom corner in as you roll. You will have to paste the join together with a couple of crushed grains of rice. Repeat with the other pieces of nori.

tuna sesame blocks

Sesame oil comes in 2 sorts:
pale unroasted oil, usually Middle Eastern, or dark roasted oil, usually from Asia or China.
The roasted oil has a much stronger flavor. *MAKES 12 PIECES*

3¹/₄ x 2¹/₂-inch (8 x 6-cm) piece center-cut
tuna fillet (ask for a piece
³/₄ inch/2 cm thick)
2 tsp sesame oil
2 tbsp toasted sesame seeds
3 small sheets of nori,
cut into 4 strips lengthwise
2 tbsp oil

Cut the tuna into 12 cubes and roll the cubes in the sesame oil, followed by the sesame seeds.

Roll each cube in a sheet of nori, trimming off any excess so that the nori goes round the tuna once with only a little overlap. Moisten the edge of the nori with a little water to stick it down.

Heat the oil in a skillet and put the cubes into the skillet, standing them up on one nori-free end. Cook for 2 minutes, then turn over to cook the other nori-free end. The sesame seeds should be a dark brown, but not burned, and the tuna should have cooked most of the way through, leaving a rare patch in the middle. If you prefer your tuna fully cooked, just cook each end for a little longer.

seafood sushi

LOBSTER, shrimp, scallops, squid, and crab are used to create a tantalizing range of dishes in Part Two. Sushi's versatility is apparent in this selection of boat, rolled, scattered, and pressed sushi recipes.

shrimp rolls

Avocado used for sushi should be firm and ripe, but not overripe, or the pressure used to roll the sushi will squash it. *MAKES 12 PIECES*

2 red bell peppers
1 small ripe avocado, cut into slices
8 large cooked shelled shrimp
salt and pepper

Preheat the oven to 400°F/200°C. Put the bell peppers in a roasting pan and cook them for 30 minutes, or until the skins have browned and started to puff away from the flesh. Cool, then pull off the skins. Cut each bell pepper in half and discard the stem, seeds, and membrane.

Lay out each bell pepper half on a board and make a pile of avocado slices along one end. Add 2 shrimp to each and season with salt and pepper. Roll up the bell peppers tightly and wrap each roll tightly in plastic wrap, then chill for 30 minutes.

Carefully unwrap the plastic wrap from the bell peppers and trim each end until it is straight. Cut each roll into 3 pieces with a wet, very sharp knife. Turn the pieces on end and arrange them on a plate.

shrimp & avocado skewers

Nori sheets are made from dried laver seaweed and come in different sizes. If you can find them in both large and small sizes, use whichever is appropriate to the recipe. If you can find only one size, adjust the recipe to suit the size of the sheet. Buy nori sheets that are marked "toasted" if possible. Untoasted sheets are not as crisp or highly flavored, but you can toast them by passing the non-shiny side over a naked flame. When rolling the sheets, always put them on the mat shiny-side down. *MAKES 6*

1 quantity freshly cooked sushi rice (see page 78)
6 small sheets of toasted nori
1 tbsp Japanese mayonnaise
1 tsp lemon zest

12 cooked jumbo shrimp, shelled and deveined
2 ripe avocados, cut into strips
2-inch/5-cm piece of cucumber, peeled and cut into batons
6 bamboo skewers

Divide the rice into 6 equal portions. Put a sheet of nori shiny-side down on a rolling mat with the longest end toward you. Using wet hands, spread 1 portion of the rice in an even layer on the nori, leaving 3/4 inch/2 cm of nori visible at the end farthest away from you. Don't squash the rice or make the layer too thick—you should be able to see the nori through the rice.

Mix the mayonnaise with the lemon zest and then spread some onto the rice at the end nearest to you. Lay 2 shrimp end to end on top of the mayonnaise, then put a line of avocado next to them. Lay a line of cucumber next to the avocado.

To roll the sushi, fold the mat over, starting at the end where the ingredients are and tucking in the end of the nori to start the roll. Keep rolling, lifting up the mat as you go and keeping the pressure even but gentle until you have finished the roll. Moisten the top edge of the nori with water to seal the sushi roll closed. Don't worry if anything falls out of the sides; just push it back in. Remove the roll from the mat and cut into 4 even-size pieces with a wet, very sharp knife. If you don't use a sharp knife, the roll will squash as you cut it. Lay the pieces on their side. Push each bamboo skewer through 4 pieces.

scattered sushi
with shrimp, crab & avocado

If you would like to keep the shrimp straight so that they are easier to arrange in lines, push a skewer through their length before cooking to stop them curling up. *SERVES 4*

6 large raw shrimp, shelled and deveined

1 tbsp oil

1 cooked prepared crab

1 quantity freshly cooked sushi rice
  (see page 78)

juice and zest of 1 lemon

1 ripe avocado, cut into strips

1/2 cucumber, peeled and cut into slices

Cook the shrimp by frying them for 2 minutes on each side in the oil. Once they are cooked, cool and cut in half lengthwise. Lift the crabmeat out of the shell.

Mix the sushi rice with the lemon juice and lemon zest.

Divide the rice between 4 wooden or ceramic bowls—they should be about 3/4 inch/2 cm full. Arrange the shrimp, crab, avocado, and cucumber on top of the rice.

to serve

pickled ginger

wasabi paste

lemon wedges

lemon pepper crab sushi boats

To make a really quick and easy topping, use a can of lemon pepper tuna instead of the crab. Drain the tuna of any excess liquid and stir it well before use. *MAKES 8 PIECES*

1 small cooked prepared crab

1 tsp grated lemon zest

1 tsp black pepper

2 tbsp Japanese mayonnaise

salt

$^{1}/_{3}$ quantity freshly cooked sushi rice (see page 78)

2 small sheets of toasted nori, each cut into 4 strips lengthwise

juice of 1 lemon

Lift the crabmeat out of the shell and mix with the lemon, black pepper, and mayonnaise. Season with salt to taste.

Divide the rice into 8 batches. Dampen your hands to stop the rice sticking, then shape each batch of the rice into an oval using your hands. Carefully wrap a strip of nori around each piece of rice and trim off any excess, then stick the seaweed together at the join using a couple of crushed grains of rice.

Top each sushi boat with some of the crab mixture and squeeze over a few drops of lemon juice. Serve the sushi straightaway with pickled ginger, wasabi paste, and lemon wedges.

crab, asparagus
& shiitake rolls with ponzu sauce

Shiitake mushrooms can be bought both fresh and dried. If you can't find the fresh mushrooms, soak dried ones in boiling water for 30 minutes, then drain and squeeze dry. You can now cook them according to the recipe. *MAKES 24 PIECES*

6 asparagus spears

1 tbsp oil

6 shiitake mushrooms, sliced

1 quantity freshly cooked sushi rice (see page 78)

6 small sheets of toasted nori

wasabi paste

6 crab sticks, split in half lengthwise

ponzu sauce

3 tbsp mirin

2 tbsp rice vinegar

1 tbsp light soy sauce

2 tbsp bonito flakes

4 tbsp lemon juice

Lay the asparagus spears flat in a skillet filled with simmering water and cook until tender when pierced with the tip of a knife. Cut into 3¹/₂-inch/9-cm lengths and let cool.

Heat the oil in a skillet and cook the mushrooms over medium heat for 5 minutes, or until completely soft.

To make the Ponzu Sauce, put all the ingredients in a small pan and bring to a boil. Once they have boiled, turn off the heat and cool the sauce.

Divide the rice into 6 equal portions. Put a sheet of nori shiny-side down on a rolling mat with the longest end toward you. Using wet hands, spread 1 portion of the rice in an even layer on the nori, leaving ³/₄ inch/2 cm of nori visible at the end farthest away from you.

Spread a small amount of wasabi onto the rice at the end nearest you. Lay an asparagus spear on top of the wasabi, then put 2 pieces of crab next to it. Add a line of mushrooms.

To roll the sushi, fold the mat over, starting at the end where the ingredients are and tucking in the end of the nori to start the roll. Keep rolling, lifting up the mat as you go and keeping the pressure even but gentle until you have finished the roll. Moisten the top edge of the nori with water to seal the sushi roll closed.

Remove the roll from the mat and cut it into 4 even-size pieces with a wet, very sharp knife. Arrange the rolls on a plate. Repeat with the remaining ingredients, and then serve with the Ponzu Sauce.

california rolls

Crab sticks, sometimes called imitation crab sticks, are widely available. Made from fish or seafood, they are neatly shaped logs with a pink strip down one side. Crab sticks are found in California rolls, but because of their neat shape they are also very useful for other types of rolled sushi. *MAKES 24 PIECES*

1 quantity freshly cooked sushi rice (see page 78)
6 small sheets of toasted nori
wasabi paste, plus extra to garnish

¹/₂ ripe avocado, cut into batons
6 crab sticks, split in half lengthwise
2-inch/5-cm piece of cucumber, peeled and cut into batons

Divide the rice into 6 equal portions. Put a sheet of nori shiny-side down on a rolling mat with the longest end toward you. Using wet hands, spread 1 portion of the rice in an even layer on the nori, leaving ³/₄ inch/2 cm of nori visible at the end farthest away from you. Don't squash the rice or make the layer too thick—you should be able to see the nori through the rice.

Spread a small amount of wasabi onto the rice at the end nearest you. Lay 2 avocado batons down on top of the wasabi, keeping them parallel to the edge of the nori nearest you, then put 2 pieces of crab next to them. Add a line of cucumber batons.

To roll the sushi, fold the mat over, starting at the end where the ingredients are and tucking in the end of the nori to start the roll. Keep rolling, lifting up the mat as you go and keeping the pressure even but gentle until you have finished the roll. Moisten the top edge of the nori with water to seal the sushi roll closed. Don't worry if anything falls out of the sides; just push it back in. The edges may well look ragged, but don't worry.

Remove the roll from the mat and cut it into 4 even-size pieces with a wet, very sharp knife. If you don't use a sharp knife, the roll will squash as you cut it. Arrange the rolls on a plate. Repeat with the remaining ingredients. Serve with shoyu, pickled ginger, and some extra wasabi paste.

to serve
shoyu (Japanese soy sauce)
pickled ginger

inside-out
california rolls

Sesame seeds are available raw and toasted, the toasted ones having a more pronounced flavor. If you can find only raw ones, dry-fry them in a hot skillet until they brown and start to smell aromatic. *MAKES 24 PIECES*

Divide the rice into 6 equal portions. Line a rolling mat with plastic wrap to prevent the rice sticking to it. Put a sheet of nori shiny-side down on the mat with the longest end toward you. Using wet hands, spread 1 portion of the rice in an even layer on the nori, leaving no gaps, then turn the nori over so that the mat is against the rice.

Put some avocado in a layer at one end of the roll, keeping it parallel to the edge nearest you, and lay 2 pieces of crab in a line beside it. Put a line of cucumber next to them.

To roll the sushi, fold the mat over, starting at the end where the ingredients are and tucking in the end of the nori to start the roll. Keep rolling, lifting up the mat as you go and keeping the pressure even but gentle until you have finished the roll. Put the sesame seeds on a plate and roll the sushi in them to coat the rice.

Remove the roll from the mat and cut it into 4 even-size pieces with a wet, very sharp knife. If you don't use a sharp knife, the roll will squash as you cut it. Arrange the pieces on a plate. Do the same with the remaining ingredients.

1 quantity freshly cooked sushi rice (see page 78)
6 small sheets of toasted nori
1/4 ripe avocado, cut into strips
6 crab sticks, split in half lengthwise
2-inch/5-cm piece of cucumber, peeled and cut into batons
3 tbsp toasted sesame seeds

pressed california sushi

Wasabi is usually bought as a paste or powder and is made from a grated root. The powder can be mixed to a paste and is often of a better quality than the tubes of paste. Wasabi is very strong, so be careful not to use too much. *MAKES 15 PIECES*

½ quantity freshly cooked sushi rice
(see page 78)
2 tbsp Japanese mayonnaise
1 tsp toasted sesame seeds
½ avocado, cut into strips
4 crab sticks, sliced on the diagonal, or the
flesh from a cooked, prepared crab
½ cucumber, peeled and cut into
very thin slices

Oil an *oshi waku* or 7-inch/18-cm loose-bottomed square cake pan and line it with a piece of plastic wrap so that the plastic wrap hangs over the edges. This is to help you pull the sushi out afterward. Pack the tin 1¼ inches/3 cm full with the rice. Spread a layer of mayonnaise on top of the rice and sprinkle over the sesame seeds. Arrange the avocado, crab, and cucumber in thick, diagonal strips on top of the rice. Cover the top of the rice with a strip of plastic wrap, then put another cake pan on top and weight down with something heavy, such as a couple of cans of tomatoes.

Chill the sushi for 15 minutes, then take off the pan and weights. Loosen the sides of the cake pan and pull out the sushi. Cut the sushi into about 15 pieces with a wet, sharp knife. Serve with pickled ginger and wasabi paste.

to serve

pickled ginger

wasabi paste

scattered sushi with lobster & wasabi mayonnaise

Lobster can be bought cooked, but if you plan on cooking it yourself, make sure that you buy it live. *SERVES 4*

1 cooked lobster

2 tbsp Japanese mayonnaise

1 tsp wasabi paste

1 quantity freshly cooked sushi rice
    (see page 78)

1 tbsp pickled ginger, very finely chopped

1/2 cucumber, cut into slices

1 ripe avocado, cut into slices

Take the meat out of the lobster shell in as big pieces as you can. If your lobster is whole, the best way to do this is to twist off the head and halve the body down the center with a big sharp knife or cleaver. The claws will have to be smashed open to get at the meat. Cover them with a cloth and hit them hard with a rolling pin.

Mix the mayonnaise with the wasabi. Mix the sushi rice with the finely chopped pickled ginger.

Divide the rice between 4 wooden or ceramic bowls—they should be about 3/4 inch/2 cm full. Arrange the lobster, cucumber, and avocado on top of the rice and drizzle the wasabi mayonnaise into the gaps. Garnish with pickled ginger and a small mound of wasabi.

to garnish

wasabi paste

pickled ginger

salt & pepper squid hand rolls

Sichuan pepper is not a true pepper, but is made from the red berries of the prickly ash tree. The Japanese version is called sansho and is interchangeable. *MAKES 6 PIECES*

12 squid rings
4 tbsp all-purpose flour
1 tsp Sichuan pepper or black pepper, crushed
1 tsp sea salt, crushed
oil, for frying
3 large sheets of toasted nori, halved
1/4 quantity freshly cooked sushi rice (see page 78)
4 tbsp Japanese mayonnaise

Pull any membranes off the squid rings, then cut each one in half. Mix the flour with the Sichuan pepper and salt and put it with the squid in a plastic bag. Shake well until the squid is thoroughly coated.

Heat about 3/4 inch/2 cm of oil in a wok until it is very hot, then add the squid in batches and cook, stirring, for a minute, or until the coating is browned. Drain on paper towels to get rid of any excess oil.

Lay a piece of nori out on the counter and put some rice on the sheet. Spread the rice out evenly so that it takes up the bottom two-thirds of the sheet. Lay a sixth of the salt and pepper squid on the rice, then drizzle over a little mayonnaise. Roll the nori into a cone, folding the bottom corner in as you roll. You will have to paste the join together with a couple of crushed grains of rice. Repeat with the other pieces of nori.

cocktail scattered
sushi on scallop shells

Scallops can be bought on the shell and the fish dealer may even
be able to clean them for you. Packets of scallop shells can also be bought
for decorative purposes. *MAKES 8 SHELLS*

8 scallops with their shells
1 tbsp oil
juice and zest of 1/2 lime
1/3 quantity freshly cooked sushi rice
(see page 78)
handful of cilantro leaves

Remove the scallops from their shells and clean
and keep the shells for serving. Clean the scallops
by pulling off the small, white shiny muscle and its
membrane. Leave the roe attached, but check to
see if there is a black vein that needs to be cut
off—this is easiest with a pair of scissors. Heat the
oil in a skillet and briefly cook the scallops on both
sides until they are lightly browned and cooked
through. Squeeze a little of the lime juice over
each scallop and cool.

Mix the sushi rice with the remaining lime
juice and zest.

Divide the rice between 8 scallop shells—
make a small, neat mound on each one and flatten
the top a little. Arrange a scallop and a few cilantro
leaves on top of the rice in each shell, then garnish
with a piece of pickled ginger, a tiny mound
of wasabi, and a dollop of mayonnaise. Serve on
a platter with a pile of chopsticks.

to garnish

pickled ginger

wasabi paste

3 tbsp Japanese mayonnaise

scallop, mayonnaise, potato & sesame rolls

This recipe also works with firm white fish or salmon fillets. Use thick slices of fillet and fry, broil, or steam until it is just cooked. *MAKES 24 PIECES*

Cook the potatoes in a pan of boiling salted water for 20–30 minutes, or until tender. Mash with the butter and season well with the salt and pepper. Chill for 30 minutes, or until the mash is very firm.

Heat the oil in a skillet and cook the scallops for 2–3 minutes on both sides. Slice them thinly into 3 coin-shaped pieces and season with salt to taste.

Divide the mash into 6 equal portions. Put a sheet of nori shiny-side down on a rolling mat with the longest end toward you and mound 1 portion of the mash on the bottom third of the nori. Spread some mayonnaise on top, then sprinkle on some sesame seeds. Add a sixth of the scallop slices.

To roll the sushi, fold the mat over, starting at the end where the ingredients are and tucking in the end of the nori to start the roll. Keep rolling, lifting up the mat as you go and keeping the pressure even but gentle until you have finished the roll. Moisten the top edge of the nori with water to seal the sushi roll closed.

2 large potatoes, peeled
and cut into fourths
2 tbsp butter
salt and pepper
1 tbsp olive oil
8 large scallops, cleaned
6 sheets of toasted nori
2 tbsp Japanese mayonnaise
2 tbsp toasted sesame seeds

Remove the roll from the mat and cut it into 4 even-size pieces with a wet, very sharp knife. Turn the pieces on end and arrange them on a plate. Repeat with the remaining ingredients.

meat & poultry sushi

THOUGH sushi brings to mind fish and seafood, it is very versatile and may also encompass meat and poultry dishes. Beef, pork, chicken, and duck are all used in the mouthwatering dishes that follow in Part Three.

scattered sushi with
soy-glazed steak

Mirin is a sweet rice wine that acts as a flavoring. It is used to make sushi rice and gives
a luster to the rice as well as adding flavor. Hon mirin and shin mirin are the 2 varieties,
the difference being that hon mirin contains more alcohol. *SERVES 4*

8 dried shiitake mushrooms

2-inch/5-cm piece of daikon, peeled

2-inch/5-cm piece of carrot, peeled

1 tbsp soy sauce

1 tsp mirin

1 tsp brown sugar

7 oz/200 g tenderloin steak, trimmed

1 quantity freshly cooked sushi rice

(see page 78)

Soak the mushrooms in boiling water for 20 minutes, then simmer them in the same liquid for 3 minutes. Lift them out and squeeze them dry. Chop 4 mushrooms into small pieces and halve the rest. Shred the daikon and carrot using the finest setting on a mandoline or a very sharp knife. If you

are using a knife, then cut the daikon and carrot into long, thin slices and cut each slice along its length as finely as you can.

Preheat the broiler to its highest setting. Mix the soy sauce, mirin, and brown sugar together and brush the mixture all over the steak. Broil the steak for 3 minutes on each side, then let it rest for a minute. Slice into strips.

Mix the sushi rice with the chopped shiitake mushrooms.

Fill 1 large or 4 small wooden or ceramic bowls or plates with the rice—they should be about 3/4 inch/2 cm full. Arrange the steak and halved mushrooms on top of the rice and add a neat pile of shredded daikon and carrot to each bowl. Garnish with some nori strips and serve.

to garnish

strips of toasted nori

inside-out rolls
with beef teriyaki

This recipe works equally well with chicken, salmon, or slices of tofu. Use the same weight of any of the above and follow the recipe in the same way. *MAKES 24 PIECES*

5¹/₂ oz/150 g tenderloin steak, trimmed

2 tbsp teriyaki sauce

1 tbsp oil

1 quantity freshly cooked sushi rice

(see page 78)

6 small sheets of toasted nori

2 scallions, shredded

3 tbsp toasted sesame seeds

Beat the steak out flat using a meat mallet or rolling pin to make it thinner and more tender. Coat the steak in the teriyaki sauce and let it marinate for an hour. Heat the oil in a skillet and cook the steak for 3 minutes on each side. Cut the steak into thin strips.

Divide the rice into 6 equal portions. Line a rolling mat with plastic wrap to prevent the rice sticking to it. Put a sheet of nori shiny-side down on the mat with the longest end toward you. Using wet hands, spread 1 portion of the rice in an even layer on the nori, leaving no gaps, then turn the nori over so that the mat is against the rice. Put a sixth of the beef teriyaki in a layer at one long end

of the roll, then top with a layer of scallion and sprinkle with a few sesame seeds.

To roll the sushi, fold the mat over, starting at the end where the ingredients are and tucking in the end of the nori to start the roll. Keep rolling, lifting up the mat as you go and keeping the pressure even but gentle until you have finished the roll. Put the remaining sesame seeds on a plate and roll the sushi in them to coat the rice.

Remove the roll from the mat and cut it into 4 even-size pieces with a wet, sharp knife. If you don't use a sharp knife, the roll will squash as you cut it. Turn the pieces on end and arrange them on a plate. Repeat with the remaining ingredients.

chicken
teriyaki rolls

Teriyaki sauce is a widely available flavoring, or cook-in sauce.
Made from soy sauce, mirin, sake, sugar, and ginger,
it gives food a glossy coating. *MAKES 24 PIECES*

1 chicken breast, cut into strips

2 tbsp teriyaki sauce

1 tbsp oil

1 quantity freshly cooked sushi rice

(see page 78)

6 small sheets of toasted nori

2-inch/5-cm piece of cucumber, peeled and

cut into batons

Preheat the broiler to its highest setting. Toss the chicken in the teriyaki sauce and then the oil and lay out on a foil-lined broiler pan. Broil the chicken strips on both sides for about 4 minutes, then put into a bowl with any cooking juices and let cool.

Divide the rice into 6 equal portions. Put a sheet of nori shiny-side down on a rolling mat with the longest end toward you. Using wet hands, spread 1 portion of the rice in an even layer on the nori, leaving 3/4 inch/2 cm of nori visible at the end farthest away from you. Don't squash the rice or make the layer too thick—you should be able to see the nori through the rice.

Lay the chicken strips in an even line onto the rice at the end nearest to you. Then add a line of cucumber batons.

To roll the sushi, fold the mat over, starting at the end where the ingredients are and tucking in the end of the nori to start the roll. Keep rolling, lifting up the mat as you go and keeping the pressure even but gentle until you have finished the roll. Moisten the top edge of the nori with water to seal the sushi roll closed. Don't worry if anything falls out of the sides; just push it back in. The edges may well look ragged, but don't worry.

Remove the roll from the mat and cut it into 4 even-size pieces with a wet, very sharp knife. Turn the pieces on end and arrange them on a plate. Repeat with the remaining ingredients. Serve with shoyu, wasabi, and pickled ginger.

to serve

shoyu (Japanese soy sauce)

wasabi paste

pickled ginger

pork tonkatsu rolls

Tonkatsu crumbs are toasted bread crumbs, also called "panko," which are used to coat the pork fillets before cooking them. They absorb less grease than normal bread crumbs, but you can use commercial pre-toasted bread crumbs instead. *MAKES 24 PIECES*

2 tbsp all-purpose flour

1 egg, lightly beaten

4 tbsp tonkatsu crumbs or dried white bread crumbs

7 oz/200 g pork fillet, cut into thin slices

4 tbsp oil

1 quantity freshly cooked sushi rice (see page 78)

6 small sheets of toasted nori

2 tbsp Japanese mayonnaise

Put the flour, egg, and crumbs in separate bowls. One by one, dust each piece of pork in the flour and dip it in the egg, then finally press it into the crumbs. Lay the breaded pork on a plate and chill for 20 minutes.

Heat the oil in a skillet and cook the pork on both sides until the crumbs are a golden brown. It won't take long, as the slices are quite thin. Cut the slices into strips.

Divide the rice into 6 equal portions. Put a sheet of nori shiny-side down on a rolling mat with the longest end toward you. Using wet hands, spread 1 portion of the rice in an even layer on the nori, leaving 3/4 inch/2 cm of nori visible at the end farthest away from you.

Spread the mayonnaise onto the rice at the end nearest you. Lay a sixth of the pork strips on top of the mayonnaise in a line.

To roll the sushi, fold the mat over, starting at the end where the ingredients are and tucking in the end of the nori to start the roll. Keep rolling, lifting up the mat as you go and keeping the pressure even but gentle until you have finished the roll. Moisten the top edge of the nori with water to seal the sushi roll closed.

Remove the roll from the mat and cut it into 4 even-size pieces with a wet, very sharp knife. Turn the pieces on end and arrange them on a plate. Repeat with the remaining ingredients. Serve with shoyu, wasabi, and pickled ginger.

to serve
shoyu (Japanese soy sauce)
wasabi paste
pickled ginger

duck & hoisin
hand rolls

Barbecued duck can be bought from Chinese restaurants, where you will see it hanging in the window. You can also buy it from supermarkets alongside the Chinese ready-meals. A roasted duck breast will also work for this recipe. *MAKES 6 PIECES*

¹/4 barbecued or Peking duck

4 tbsp hoisin or plum sauce

3 large sheets of toasted nori, halved

¹/4 quantity freshly cooked sushi rice

(see page 78)

2 scallions, halved and shredded,

and extra to garnish

Pull the flesh and skin off the duck in big pieces, then slice these into strips. If you have lots of skin, just keep the crispiest bits. Get rid of any excess fat. Toss the duck flesh and skin with half the hoisin or plum sauce.

Lay a piece of nori out on the counter and put some rice on the sheet. Spread the rice out evenly so that it takes up the bottom two-thirds of the sheet. Lay a sixth of the duck, duck skin, and scallion on the rice, then drizzle over a little more of the hoisin or plum sauce. Roll the nori into a cone, folding the bottom corner in as you roll. You will have to paste the join together with a couple of crushed grains of rice. Repeat with the other pieces of nori. Serve garnished with shredded scallions.

rice, vegetables & tempura

THE following final section in the book includes the recipe for the most important ingredient in sushi: the rice. It also features the recipe for another Japanese staple: Miso Soup. These are followed by a number of exquisitely presented tempura and vegetable dishes, all designed to delight your senses.

sushi rice

Rice is the most important ingredient in sushi. There are several brands of sushi rice on the market. All are white and short-grain, and marked specifically "sushi rice." If you can't find sushi rice, use another type of short-grained white rice.

9 oz/250 g sushi rice
scant 1¹/₂ cups water
1 piece of kombu (optional)
2 tbsp sushi rice seasoning

Wash the sushi rice under cold running water until the water running through it is completely clear, then drain the rice. Put the rice in a pan with the water and the *kombu* (if you are using it), then cover and bring to a boil as quickly as you can. Remove the *kombu*, then turn the heat down and simmer for 10 minutes. Turn off the heat and let the rice stand for 15 minutes. Do not at any point take the lid off the pan once you have removed the *kombu*.

Put the hot rice in a *sushi-oke* (large, very shallow bowl) and pour the sushi rice seasoning evenly over the surface of the rice. Now you will need to use both hands, one to mix the seasoning into the rice with quick cutting strokes using a *shamoji* (spatula) and the other to fan the sushi rice in order to cool it down as quickly as you can. Mix the seasoning in carefully—you do not want to break a single rice grain.

The sushi rice should look shiny and be at room temperature when you are ready to use it.

miso soup

Dashi is a soup stock made from bonito flakes, kombu, and water. It is available as dashi powder and just needs to be mixed with water. *SERVES 4*

4 cups water

2 teaspoons powdered dashi

6 oz/175 g block soft tofu, cut into
¹/₂ -inch/1-cm cubes

4 shiitake or white mushrooms, sliced

4 tbsp miso

2 scallions, chopped

Put the water and dashi in a pan and bring it to a boil. Add the tofu and mushrooms, then turn down the heat and simmer gently for 3 minutes. Stir in the miso and simmer gently until it has dissolved completely. Turn off the heat, then add the scallion and serve straightaway—the longer you leave miso, the more it will settle and separate out.

to serve

tempura dipping sauce

vegetable & tofu tempura

Tofu is sold in cartons in most supermarkets, but you will find a much wider variety in Japanese or Chinese stores. Silken tofu is very soft and breaks easily, but has a wonderful texture. Firm tofu is harder and easier to use. There is a Japanese version called *nigari*. **SERVES 4**

1 potato, peeled

1/4 butternut squash, peeled

1 small sweet potato, peeled

1 small eggplant

5 1/2 oz/150 g package tempura mix

6 green beans, trimmed

1 red bell pepper, cut into thick strips

6 whole shiitake or white mushrooms, stems trimmed

1 head broccoli, broken into florets

12 oz/350 g block firm tofu, cubed

oil, for deep-frying

few drops of sesame oil

Cut the potato, squash, sweet potato, and egg-plant into 1/2-inch/1-cm thick pieces.

Combine the tempura mix with the amount of water described in the package directions until you have a lumpy batter full of air bubbles. Do not try to make the batter smooth, or it will be heavy; and make sure you use it straightaway, or it will settle.

Drop all the prepared vegetables and tofu into the batter.

Heat the oil in a deep-fryer to 350–375°F/180–190°C, or until a cube of bread browns in 30 seconds. Add a few drops of sesame oil.

Add the tempura in batches of 2–3. If you add too many pieces at one time, the oil temperature will drop and the batter will be soggy. When the tempura pieces are a very light golden color, which should take only 2–3 minutes, take them out and try to drain off as much oil as possible. Leave them to drain on paper towels for 30 seconds to blot up more oil.

Serve very hot with the dipping sauce.

mediterranean
pressed sushi

Weight down pressed sushi by applying a firm, even pressure so that the decorative layer stays flat. The ingredients can be arranged in the bottom and the rice pressed on top, or the other way around. *MAKES 15 PIECES*

2 red bell peppers
¹/₂ quantity freshly cooked sushi rice
(see page 78)
oil, for brushing
3¹/₂ oz/100 g mozzarella, cut into thin slices
4 sun-dried tomatoes in oil,
drained and cut into strips
handful of small basil leaves

Preheat the oven to 400°F/200°C. Put the bell peppers in a roasting pan and cook them for 30 minutes, or until the skins have browned and started to puff away from the flesh. Cool, then pull off the skins. Cut each bell pepper in half and discard the stem, seeds, and membrane. Cut the bell peppers into strips.

Oil an *oshi waku* or 7-inch/18-cm loose-bottomed square cake pan and line it with a piece of plastic wrap so that the plastic wrap hangs over the edges. This is to help you pull the sushi out afterward. Pack the pan 1¹/4 inches/3 cm full with the rice and brush the top with a tiny amount of oil to help the toppings stick.

Arrange the bell pepper and mozzarella in thick, diagonal strips on top of the rice, alternating red sun-dried tomatoes and green basil leaves as thinner strips between the thick bell pepper and mozzarella strips. Cover the top of the rice with a strip of plastic wrap, then put another pan or flat tray on top and weight down with something heavy, such as conventional weights or a couple of cans of tomatoes.

Chill the sushi for 15 minutes. Take off the pan and weights, then loosen the sides of the cake pan and pull out the sushi. Cut the sushi into about 15 pieces with a wet, sharp knife.

green bean sushi boats

Bean shredders are the best way to shred beans into long strips.
They are small plastic frames filled with 5 or 6 blades.

MAKES 8 PIECES

20 green beans, trimmed
and finely sliced

1 tbsp sesame oil

1 tbsp toasted sesame seeds

salt and pepper

1 tsp grated lemon zest

¹/₃ quantity freshly cooked sushi rice (see
page 78)

2 small sheets of toasted nori, each cut into

4 strips lengthwise

wasabi paste

Put the green beans in a pan with a little water and bring to a boil. Cook for 2 minutes, then drain and toss with the sesame oil and sesame seeds. Season with salt and pepper to taste and mix in the lemon zest.

Divide the rice into 8 batches. Dampen your hands to stop the rice sticking, then shape each batch into an oval using your hands. Carefully wrap a strip of nori around each piece of rice and trim off any excess, then stick together at the join using a couple of crushed grains of rice.

Dab a little wasabi on top of each sushi boat and top with the green beans. Serve the sushi straightaway with soy sauce.

to serve

soy sauce

soba noodle rolls

Soba noodles are long, brownish-gray noodles made from buckwheat and wheat flour. They can be eaten hot or cold, as here. *MAKES 24 PIECES*

4 oz/115 g sushi-grade tuna or piece of tuna fillet

1 tbsp oil

3¹/₂ oz/100 g soba noodles, broken into pieces

1 scallion, green part only, cut into thin slices

1 tbsp light soy sauce

¹/₂ tbsp rice wine vinegar

wasabi paste

1 tbsp pickled ginger, finely chopped

6 small sheets of toasted nori

¹/₂ cucumber, peeled and finely shredded

If using a piece of tuna fillet, heat the oil in a skillet and sear the tuna on all sides for 6 minutes, or until it is almost cooked through. Cut the sushi or cooked tuna into strips.

Cook the soba noodles in a pan of boiling water until they are just cooked through, then drain and rinse under cold running water. Drain thoroughly. Gently mix the soba noodles with the scallion, soy sauce, rice wine vinegar, a little wasabi, and the pickled ginger.

Divide the noodles into 6 equal portions. Put a sheet of nori shiny-side down on a rolling mat with the longest end toward you and mound 1 portion of the noodle mixture on the bottom third of the nori. Lay a sixth of the cucumber on top, then a layer of tuna strips.

To roll the sushi, fold the mat over, starting at the end where the ingredients are and tucking in the end of the nori to start the roll. Keep rolling, lifting up the mat as you go and keeping the pressure even but gentle until you have finished the roll. Moisten the top edge of the nori with water to seal the sushi roll closed. Don't worry if anything falls out of the sides; just push it back in.

Remove the roll from the mat and cut it into 4 even-size pieces with a wet, very sharp knife. Turn the pieces on end and arrange them on a plate. Repeat the process with the remaining ingredients.

asparagus & omelet
rolls with ponzu sauce

Ponzu sauce is traditionally made with ponzu, or kalamansi, an Oriental citron variety.
Lemon or lime juice can be used instead. *MAKES 6–8 PIECES*

8 asparagus spears
4 eggs
1 tbsp water
1 tbsp mirin
1 tsp soy sauce
1/2 tbsp oil

Lay the asparagus flat in a skillet filled with simmering water and cook until tender when pierced with the tip of a knife. Let cool.

Whisk the eggs with the water, mirin, and soy sauce. Heat the oil in a nonstick skillet and pour in the egg mixture. Cook on one side until the top is just set, then add the asparagus spears by laying them in lines at one end of the skillet.

Shake the skillet to loosen the omelet. Now roll up the omelet, starting at the asparagus end, by tipping the skillet away from you so that the omelet slides up the side of the skillet. Using 2 chopsticks, fold the omelet over and keep rolling it up like a jelly roll.

Put a sheet of plastic wrap in the center of a rolling mat. Tip the omelet out onto the plastic wrap and roll it up in the mat to help it set in shape. Let cool.

Remove the roll from the mat and cut it into 3/4-inch (2-cm) pieces with a wet, very sharp knife. Turn the pieces on end and arrange them on a plate. Serve with the Ponzu Sauce for dipping.

to serve

Ponzu Sauce (see page 48)

to garnish

cucumber batons

pickled ginger

to serve

shoyu (Japanese soy sauce)

sushi bags

Aburage are wrappers made by lifting the skin off soya milk and drying it. The pouches are used to make this *inari* (stuffed) sushi. Some come dry, others are pre-seasoned. *MAKES 8 PIECES*

Put the beancurd in a bowl and pour boiling water over it to remove any excess oil, then drain and cool. Cut each piece in half and gently open out each half into a bag.

Combine the dashi stock, soy sauce, sugar, and sake in a pan and bring to a boil, then add the beancurd bags and simmer for 10–15 minutes, or until the liquid has almost all been absorbed. Remove from the heat, then drain and cool. Press any remaining liquid out of the bags with a clean dish towel—they should be moist but not wet.

Add the sesame seeds to the sushi rice and mix them in. Fill the bags with the rice mixture and fold over the tops to enclose them. Serve at room temperature.

4 aburage (fried beancurd sheets)

3/4 cup dashi stock

3 tbsp soy sauce

2 tbsp superfine sugar

1 tbsp sake

1 tbsp toasted sesame seeds

1/4 quantity freshly cooked sushi rice (see page 78)

seafood tempura

Tempura mix is available in packages and just needs to be mixed with water. Don't be tempted to make a smooth batter, because a lumpier batter works better. *SERVES 4*

8 large raw shrimp, shelled and deveined

4 scallops, cleaned

8 squid rings

7 oz/200 g firm white fish fillets, cut into strips

5¹/₂ oz/150 g package tempura mix

oil, for deep-frying

few drops of sesame oil

Make little cuts on the underside of the shrimp to keep them straight while they cook. Pull any membranes off the squid rings.

Combine the tempura mix with the amount of water described on the package directions until you have a lumpy batter full of air bubbles. Do not try to make the batter smooth, or it will be heavy; and make sure you use it straightaway, or it will settle.

Drop all the seafood and fish into the batter.

Heat the oil in a deep-fryer to 350–375°F/ 180–190°C, or until a cube of bread browns in 30 seconds. Add a few drops of sesame oil to the fryer.

Add the tempura in batches of 2–3. If you add too many pieces at one time, the oil temperature will drop and the batter will be soggy. When the tempura pieces are a very light golden color, which should take only 2–3 minutes, take them out and try to drain off as much oil as possible. Let them drain on paper towels for 30 seconds to blot up more oil.

Serve this dish very hot with the tempura dipping sauce.

to serve

tempura dipping sauce

index